CHOCOLATE
HEAVEN

Consultant Editor:
Valerie Ferguson

LORENZ BOOKS

Contents

Introduction   4

Types of Chocolate   6

Techniques   8

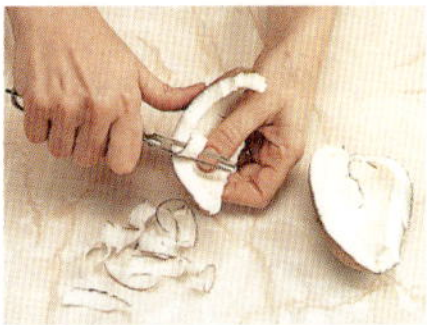

Recipes

    Tea-time Treats   10
    Cookies, Brownies & Muffins   20 
    Ice Creams, Sorbets & Mousses   30
    Hot Desserts   38
    Special Occasion Desserts   46

Index   64

Introduction

Chocolate is one of the world's best-loved foods. It is an ingredient with a long and impressive pedigree: for centuries the Aztecs drank a bitter, frothy drink called 'chocolatl', made of roasted cocoa beans mixed with water or wine. Cocoa beans, which are actually the seeds of the cacao tree, were then introduced to Europe in the sixteenth century, and cocoa became a food of kings.

Its true potential was not exploited until the early nineteenth century when the chocolate press was invented in Holland, but from that point onwards, chocolate has gone from strength to strength. Chocolate is now available in countless forms and varieties, and is used as a flavouring in every conceivable dessert and sweet. Cocoa butter, which is retained in solid chocolate, is a rich source of energy.

This book is for all lovers of chocolate. It contains a glorious array of fabulous desserts and sweet indulgences – cakes, pies, mousses, ice creams, cookies, brownies, muffins and truffles galore – using chocolate in every guise. The recipes are special enough to share with friends, or give as gifts, but be sure to make an extra batch to enjoy yourself – they are truly irresistible.

Types of Chocolate

PLAIN DARK CHOCOLATE
Often called "luxury", "bitter" or "continental" chocolate, this has a high percentage of cocoa solids – around 75 per cent – with little or no added sugar. Many people find plain dark chocolate too bitter for eating, but its rich, intense flavour and good dark colour make it an ideal ingredient in desserts or cakes.

PLAIN CHOCOLATE
Ordinary plain chocolate is the most widely available chocolate for use in cooking. It contains between 30 and 70 per cent cocoa solids, so check the label before you buy. The higher the content of cocoa solids, the better the chocolate flavour will be.

MILK CHOCOLATE
This contains powdered or condensed milk and generally has around 20 per cent cocoa solids. The flavour is mild and sweet. Although this is the most popular eating chocolate, it is not as suitable as plain chocolate for melting and cooking purposes.

WHITE CHOCOLATE
This does not contain any cocoa solids, but gets its flavour from cocoa butter. It is sweet, and the better quality white chocolate is quite rich and smooth. White chocolate must be melted with care as it does not withstand heat as well as plain chocolate and is liable to stiffen if allowed to get too hot.

plain chocolate

cocoa

plain dark chocolate

organic chocolate

milk chocolate

*chocolate-flavour
cake covering*

*chocolate
chips*

*white
chocolate*

*chocolate
chunks*

COCOA

This is made from the pure cocoa mass
after most of the cocoa butter has been
extracted. The mass is roasted, then
ground to make a powder. It is
probably the most economical way of
giving puddings and baked goods a
chocolate flavour.

CHOCOLATE CHIPS

These are small pieces of chocolate of
uniform size, convenient for stirring
directly into biscuit dough or cake
mixture, or for melting. They contain
fewer cocoa solids than ordinary
chocolate, and are available in plain
dark, plain, milk and white.

Techniques

MELTING CHOCOLATE
There are basically three ways to melt chocolate:

USING A DOUBLE BOILER
1 Fill the base of a double boiler or a saucepan about a quarter full with water. Fit the top pan or place a heatproof bowl over the pan. The water should not touch the top container. Bring the water to just below boiling point, then lower the heat to the lowest possible setting.

2 Break the chocolate into squares and place in the top pan or bowl. Let melt completely, without stirring. Keep the water at a very slow simmer.

DIRECT HEAT METHOD
This is only suitable for recipes where the chocolate is melted in plenty of other liquid, such as milk or cream. Break up the chocolate into a saucepan. Add the liquid, then heat gently, stirring occasionally, until the chocolate has melted and the mixture is smooth.

MELTING IN THE MICROWAVE
Break the chocolate into squares and place it in a microwave-proof bowl. Heat until just softened – chocolate burns easily in the microwave, so check often, remembering that chocolate retains its shape when melted in this way.

Approximate times for melting plain or milk chocolate in a 650–700 watt microwave oven:	
115 g/4 oz	2 minutes on High (100% power)
200–225 g/7–8 oz	3 minutes on High (100% power)
115 g/4 oz white chocolate	2 minutes on Medium (50% power)

TIPS FOR MELTING CHOCOLATE
• Melt chocolate slowly, as overheating will spoil both the flavour and texture.
• Avoid overheating – dark chocolate should not be heated above 49°C/120°F; milk and white chocolate should not go above 43°C/110°F.
• Never allow water or steam to come into contact with melting chocolate as this may cause it to stiffen.
• Do not cover chocolate after it has melted as condensation could cause it to stiffen.

STORING CHOCOLATE:
Chocolate keeps well if stored in a cool, dry place, away from strong-smelling foods. Check "best before" dates on the pack.

CHOCOLATE DECORATIONS
All these decorations can be made using plain, milk or white chocolate.

GRATED CHOCOLATE
Using a fine or coarse cheese grater or the grating blade of a food processor, grate a large bar of chocolate. Grated chocolate is useful for sprinkling over desserts or cakes, or coating the sides of gâteaux. If you use a cheese grater, stand it on a sheet of non-stick baking paper for extra convenience. The grated chocolate can then be easily tipped or brushed off as required.

QUICK CHOCOLATE CURLS
Use a swivel-bladed vegetable peeler to shave curls of chocolate from the whole bar. This works best when the chocolate has been allowed to reach room temperature.

CHOCOLATE CURLS
This method is for making larger chocolate curls.

1 Spread melted chocolate thinly and evenly over a marble slab or a cool, smooth work surface. Leave until it is just set.

2 Push a metal scraper or cheese slicer across the surface, at a 25° angle, to remove thin shavings of chocolate which should curl gently against the blade. If the chocolate sets too hard it may become too brittle to curl and must be gently melted again.

Simple Chocolate Cake

An easy, everyday chocolate cake which is delicious simply filled with chocolate buttercream.

Serves 6–8

INGREDIENTS
115 g/4 oz plain chocolate, broken into
    squares
45 ml/3 tbsp milk
150 g/5 oz/⅔ cup unsalted butter or
    margarine, softened
150 g/5 oz/scant 1 cup light muscovado
    sugar
3 eggs
200 g/7 oz/1¾ cups self-raising flour
15 ml/1 tbsp cocoa powder
icing sugar and cocoa powder, for dusting

FOR THE CHOCOLATE BUTTERCREAM
75 g/3 oz/6 tbsp unsalted butter or
    margarine, softened
175 g/6 oz/1½ cups icing sugar
15 ml/1 tbsp cocoa powder
2.5 ml/½ tsp vanilla essence

1 Preheat the oven to 180°C/350°F/
Gas 4. Grease two 18 cm/7 in
round sandwich cake tins and line the
base of each with non-stick baking
paper. Melt the chocolate with the
milk in a heatproof bowl set over a
pan of barely simmering water.

2 Cream the butter or margarine
with the sugar until pale and fluffy.
Add the eggs one at a time, beating
well after each. Stir in the chocolate
mixture until well combined.

3 Sift the flour and cocoa over the
mixture and fold in with a metal
spoon until evenly mixed. Scrape into
the prepared tins, smooth level and
bake for 35–40 minutes, or until well
risen and firm. Turn out on wire
racks to cool.

4 To make the chocolate buttercream,
place all the ingredients in a
large bowl. Beat well to a smooth,
spreadable consistency.

5 Sandwich the cake layers together
with the buttercream. Dust with
a mixture of icing sugar and cocoa
just before serving.

COOK'S TIP: For a richer finish,
make a double quantity of
buttercream and spread or pipe over
the top of the cake as well as using
for the filling.

Chocolate Layer Cake

The cake layers can be made ahead, wrapped and frozen for future use. Always thaw cakes completely before icing.

Serves 10–12

INGREDIENTS
cocoa powder for dusting
225 g/8 oz can cooked whole beetroot, drained and juice reserved
115 g/4 oz/8 tbsp unsalted butter, softened
500 g/1¼ lb/2½ cups (packed) light brown sugar
3 eggs
15 ml/1 tbsp vanilla essence
75 g/3 oz unsweetened chocolate, melted
275 g/10 oz/2½ cups plain flour
10 ml/2 tsp baking powder
2.5 ml/½ tsp salt
120 ml/4 fl oz/½ cup buttermilk
chocolate curls (optional)

FOR THE CHOCOLATE GANACHE FROSTING
475 ml/16 fl oz/2 cups whipping or double cream
500 g/1¼ lb fine quality plain chocolate, chopped
15 ml/1 tbsp vanilla essence

1 Preheat oven to 180°C/350°F/ Gas 4. Grease two 23 cm/9 in cake tins and dust the base and sides with cocoa. Grate the beetroot and add it to the juice. With an electric mixer, beat the butter, brown sugar, eggs and vanilla for 3–5 minutes, until pale and fluffy. Reduce the speed and beat in the chocolate.

2 Sift the flour, baking powder and salt into a bowl. On a low speed, alternately beat in the flour mixture (in quarters) and the buttermilk (in thirds).

3 Add the beetroot mixture and beat for 1 minute. Divide between the tins and bake for 30–35 minutes, or until a cake tester inserted in the centre comes out clean. Cool for 10 minutes, unmould and cool completely.

4 To make the frosting, heat the cream in a heavy-based saucepan over a medium heat until it just begins to boil, stirring occasionally.

5 Off the heat, add in the chocolate, stirring constantly until melted and smooth. Stir in the vanilla. Strain into a bowl and refrigerate, stirring every 10 minutes, for about 1 hour, until spreadable.

6 Assemble the cake. Place one layer on a serving plate and spread with one third of the ganache. Place the second layer over and spread the remaining ganache over the top and side of the cake. If using, top with the chocolate curls. Allow the ganache to set for 20–30 minutes, then refrigerate before serving.

Marbled Chocolate & Peanut Butter Cake

This cake cannot be tested with a cake tester because the peanut butter remains soft in the centre. Rely on the fingertip method: the cake should spring back when touched after 50–60 minutes.

Serves 12–14

INGREDIENTS

115 g/4 oz plain chocolate, chopped
225 g/8 oz/1 cup unsalted butter, softened
225 g/8 oz/1 cup smooth or chunky peanut butter
200 g/7 oz/1 cup granulated sugar
225 g/8 oz/1 cup (packed) light brown sugar
5 eggs
275 g/10 oz/2½ cups plain flour
10 ml/2 tsp baking powder
2.5 ml/½ tsp salt
120 ml/4 fl oz/½ cup milk
50 g/2 oz/⅓ cup chocolate chips

FOR THE CHOCOLATE PEANUT BUTTER GLAZE

25 g/1 oz/2 tbsp butter, cut up
25 g/1 oz/2 tbsp smooth peanut butter
45 ml/3 tbsp golden syrup
5 ml/1 tsp vanilla essence
175 g/6 oz plain chocolate, broken into pieces
15 ml/1 tbsp water

1 Preheat the oven to 180°C/350°F/ Gas 4. Generously grease and flour a 3 litre/5 pint/12 cup tube or ring mould. Melt the chocolate in the top of a double boiler over a very low heat.

2 Put the butter, peanut butter and sugars into a large mixing bowl. Beat with an electric mixer, scraping the side of the bowl occasionally, for about 3–5 minutes, until light and creamy. Add the eggs, one at a time, beating well after each addition.

3 Stir the flour, baking powder and salt in a medium bowl. Add to the butter mixture alternately with the milk until just blended.

4 Pour half the batter into another bowl. Stir the melted chocolate into one half of the batter until well blended. Stir the chocolate chips into the other half of the batter.

5 Using a large spoon, drop alternate spoonfuls of each batter into the tin. Pull a knife through to create a marbled effect; do not let the knife touch the tin or over-mix. Bake for 50–60 minutes. Cool in the tin on a wire rack for 10 minutes, then unmould on to the rack.

6 Prepare the glaze. Combine all the ingredients in a small saucepan. Melt over a low heat, stirring continuously, until well blended and smooth. Cool for 5 minutes. When slightly thickened, drizzle the glaze over the cake, allowing it to run down the side.

Chocolate Ginger Crunch Cake

Ginger adds a flicker of fire to this delectable uncooked cake. Keep one in the fridge for midnight feasts and other late-night treats.

Serves 6

INGREDIENTS
150 g/5 oz plain chocolate, broken into
    squares
50 g/2 oz/4 tbsp unsalted butter
115 g/4 oz ginger nut biscuits
4 pieces stem ginger
30 ml/2 tbsp stem ginger syrup
45 ml/3 tbsp desiccated coconut

TO DECORATE
25 g/1 oz milk chocolate
pieces of crystallized ginger

1 Grease a 15 cm/6 in flan ring; place it on a sheet of non-stick baking paper. Melt the plain chocolate with the butter in a heatproof bowl over barely simmering water. Remove from the heat.

2 Crush the ginger nut biscuits into small pieces (see Cook's Tip), and tip them into a bowl.

3 Chop the stem ginger fairly finely and mix with the crushed biscuits. Stir the biscuit mixture, ginger syrup and desiccated coconut into the melted chocolate and butter, mixing well until evenly combined.

4 Tip the mixture into the prepared flan ring and press down firmly and evenly. Chill in the fridge until set.

5 Remove the flan ring and slide the cake on to a plate. Melt the milk chocolate, drizzle it over the top of the cake and decorate with the pieces of crystallized ginger.

COOK'S TIP: Do not crumb the biscuits as you need crunchy pieces for texture. Put in a stout plastic bag and crush them with a rolling pin, or chop them in a food processor, using the pulse setting.

Bitter Marmalade Chocolate Loaf

Do not be alarmed by the amount of cream in this recipe – it is naughty but necessary, and replaces butter to make a moist dark cake, topped with a bitter-sweet sticky marmalade topping.

Serves 8

INGREDIENTS
115 g/4 oz plain chocolate,
   broken into squares
3 eggs
200 g/7 oz/1 cup caster sugar
175 ml/6 fl oz/¾ cup soured cream
200 g/7 oz/1¼ cups self-raising flour

FOR THE FILLING AND GLAZE
175 g/6 oz/⅔ cup bitter orange
   marmalade
115 g/4 oz plain chocolate,
   broken into squares
60 ml/4 tbsp soured cream
shredded orange rind,
   to decorate (optional)

1 Preheat the oven to 180°C/ 350°F/Gas 4. Lightly grease a 900 g/2 lb loaf tin and line it with non-stick baking paper. Melt the chocolate in a heatproof bowl over hot water.

2 Combine the eggs and sugar in a separate bowl. Using a hand-held electric mixer, whisk the mixture until it is thick and creamy, then stir in the soured cream and chocolate. Fold in the self-raising flour evenly.

3 Scrape the mixture into the prepared tin and bake for about 1 hour, or until well risen and firm to the touch. Cool for a few minutes in the tin, then turn out on to a wire rack and leave to cool completely.

4 Make the filling. Spoon two thirds of the marmalade into a small saucepan and melt over a gentle heat. Melt the chocolate and stir it into the marmalade with the soured cream.

5 Slice the cake across into three layers and sandwich back together with about half the marmalade filling. Spread the rest over the top of the cake and leave to set. Spoon the remaining marmalade over the cake and decorate with shredded orange rind, if using.

COOK'S TIP: If you do not particularly like marmalade, use apricot jam instead.

Black & White Ginger Florentines

These crunchy florentines can be stored in an airtight container in the fridge for up to one week.

Makes about 30

INGREDIENTS
120 ml/4 fl oz/½ cup double cream
50 g/2 oz/4 tbsp unsalted butter
90 g/3½ oz/½ cup sugar
30 ml/2 tbsp honey
150 g/5 oz/1⅔ cups flaked almonds
40 g/1½ oz/⅓ cup plain flour
2.5 ml/½ tsp ground ginger
50 g/2 oz/⅓ cup diced candied
    orange peel
65 g/2½ oz/½ cup diced stem ginger
50 g/2 oz plain chocolate,
    chopped
150 g/5 oz plain dark chocolate,
    chopped
150 g/5 oz fine quality white chocolate,
    chopped

1 Preheat oven to 180°C/350°F/ Gas 4. Lightly grease 2 large non-stick baking sheets. Stir the cream, butter, sugar and honey in a saucepan over a medium heat, until the sugar dissolves completely.

2 Bring the mixture to the boil, stirring constantly. Remove from the heat and stir in the almonds, flour and ground ginger. Stir in the orange peel, stem ginger and chopped plain chocolate.

3 Drop teaspoons of mixture on to the sheets at least 7.5 cm/3 in apart. Dip a spoon in water and use to spread as thinly as possible.

4 Bake in batches for 8–10 minutes, or until bubbling, and golden brown at the edges. Be careful not to under- or over-bake. If you wish, neaten the edges with a 7.5 cm/3 in biscuit cutter.

5 Remove from the oven and allow to cool for 10 minutes, until firm. Using a metal palette knife, transfer to a wire rack to cool completely.

6 Melt the plain dark chocolate in a saucepan over a low heat, until smooth; then cool. In the top of a double boiler over low heat, melt the white chocolate until smooth, stirring frequently. Remove from the heat and cool, stirring occasionally, for about 5 minutes, until thickened.

7 Using a palette knife, spread half the florentines with the plain dark chocolate on the flat side, swirling to create a decorative surface, and place on a wire rack, chocolate side up. Spread the remaining florentines with the white chocolate and place on a rack. Refrigerate for 10–15 minutes.

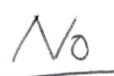

Chunky Chocolate Cookies

Do not allow these cookies to cool completely on the baking sheet or they will become too crisp and will break when you try to lift them.

Makes about 18

INGREDIENTS
175 g/6 oz plain chocolate, chopped
115 g/4 oz/ 8 tbsp unsalted butter,
   cut into pieces
2 eggs
90 g/3½ oz/½ cup sugar
50 g/2 oz/¼ cup (packed) light
   brown sugar
40 g/1½ oz/⅓ cup plain flour
25 g/1 oz/¼ cup cocoa powder
5 ml/1 tsp baking powder
10 ml/2 tsp vanilla essence
pinch of salt
115 g/4 oz/1 cup pecans, toasted and
   coarsely chopped
175 g/6 oz/1 cup plain chocolate chips
115 g/4 oz fine quality white chocolate,
   chopped into 5 mm/¼ in pieces
115 g/4 oz fine quality milk chocolate,
   chopped into 5 mm/¼ in pieces

1 Preheat oven to 160°C/325°F/ Gas 3. Grease 2 large baking sheets. Melt the plain chocolate and butter in a saucepan over a low heat, stirring frequently. Leave to cool slightly.

2 Using an electric mixer, beat the eggs and sugars for 2–3 minutes. Gradually beat in the melted chocolate. Beat in the flour, cocoa, baking powder, vanilla and salt. Stir in the nuts, chocolate chips and pieces.

3 Drop heaped tablespoons of the mixture on to the baking sheets 10 cm/4 in apart and flatten each to a round about 7.5 cm/3 in across.

4 Bake for 8–10 minutes, until the tops are shiny and cracked and the edges look crisp; do not over-bake or the cookies will break when removed from the baking sheet.

5 Remove the baking sheets to a wire rack to cool for 2 minutes, until just set, then remove the cookies to the wire rack to cool completely. Continue to bake in batches. Store in airtight containers.

Chocolate Cinnamon Doughnuts

Serve these light and luscious treats freshly made and just warm, so that the chocolate filling melts in your mouth.

Makes 16

INGREDIENTS
500 g/1¼ lb/5 cups strong
  plain flour
30 ml/2 tbsp cocoa powder
2.5 ml/½ tsp salt
1 sachet easy-blend dried yeast
300 ml/½ pint/1¼ cups
  hand-hot milk
40 g/1½ oz/3 tbsp butter,
  melted
1 egg, beaten
115 g/4 oz plain chocolate,
  broken into 16 pieces
sunflower oil for deep frying

FOR THE COATING
45 ml/3 tbsp caster sugar
15 ml/1 tbsp cocoa powder
5 ml/1 tsp ground cinnamon

1 Sift the flour, cocoa and salt into a large bowl. Stir in the yeast. Make a well in the centre and add the milk, melted butter and egg. Stir, gradually incorporating the dry ingredients to make a soft and pliable dough. Knead the dough on a lightly floured surface for about 5 minutes, until smooth and elastic. Return to the clean bowl, cover and leave in a warm place until the dough has doubled in bulk.

2 Knead the dough lightly again, then divide into 16 pieces. Shape each into a round, press a piece of plain chocolate into the centre, then fold the dough over to enclose the filling, pressing firmly to make sure the edges are sealed. Re-shape the doughnuts when sealed, if necessary.

3 Heat the oil for deep frying to 180°C/350°F, or until a cube of dried bread browns in 30–45 seconds. Deep fry the doughnuts in batches. As each doughnut rises and turns golden brown, turn it over carefully to cook the other side. Drain the cooked doughnuts well on kitchen paper.

4 Mix the sugar, cocoa and cinnamon in a shallow bowl. Toss the doughnuts in the mixture to coat them evenly. Serve warm.

Nut & Chocolate Chip Brownies

x 1·25 for 21cm sq tin.

Moist, dark and deeply satisfying – meet the ultimate chocolate brownie.

Makes 16

INGREDIENTS

188 150 g/5 oz plain chocolate,
   broken into squares
150 120 ml/4 fl oz/½ cup sunflower oil
268 215 g/7½ oz/1 cup light muscovado sugar
   2 eggs *& milk*
6¼ 5 ml/1 tsp vanilla essence
80 65 g/2½ oz/9 tbsp self-raising flour
75 60 ml/4 tbsp cocoa powder
95 75 g/3 oz/¾ cup chopped walnuts or
   pecan nuts
63 50 g/2 oz/4 tbsp milk chocolate chips

1 Preheat the oven to 180°C/350°F/
Gas 4. Lightly grease a shallow
19 cm/7½ in square cake tin. Melt the
chocolate in a bowl over hot water.

2 Beat the oil, sugar, eggs and vanilla
essence together thoroughly in a
large mixing bowl.

3 Stir in the melted chocolate,
then beat the mixture well until
it is evenly blended.

4 Sift the flour and cocoa powder
into the bowl containing the wet
ingredients and fold in thoroughly.
Stir in the chopped nuts and milk
chocolate chips, tip the mixture into
the prepared cake tin and spread it
evenly to the edges.

5 Bake for 30–35 minutes, or until
the top is firm and crusty. Allow
to cool in the tin before cutting
into 16 squares.

COOK'S TIP: These brownies will
freeze for up to 3 months in an
airtight container.

Double Chocolate Chip Muffins

The generous pieces of white and plain chocolate in these muffins make them particularly delectable.

Makes 16

INGREDIENTS
400 g/14 oz/3½ cups plain flour
15 ml/1 tbsp baking powder
30 ml/2 tbsp cocoa powder
115 g/4 oz/¾ cup dark
    muscovado sugar
2 eggs
150 ml/¼ pint/⅔ cup soured cream
150 ml/¼ pint/⅔ cup milk
60 ml/4 tbsp sunflower oil
175 g/6 oz white chocolate
175 g/6 oz plain chocolate
cocoa powder, for dusting

2 In a separate bowl, beat the eggs with the soured cream, milk and oil, then stir into the centre of the dry ingredients. Beat well, gradually incorporating the flour mixture to make a thick and creamy batter.

3 Chop both the white and the plain chocolate into small pieces, then stir into the batter mixture.

4 Spoon the mixture into the muffin cases, filling them almost to the top. Bake for 25–30 minutes, until they are well risen and firm to the touch. Cool on a wire rack, then dust with cocoa powder.

1 Preheat the oven to 190°C/375°F/ Gas 5. Place 16 paper muffin cases in muffin tins or deep bun tins. Sift the flour, baking powder and cocoa into a bowl and stir in the sugar. Make a well in the centre.

COOK'S TIP: If soured cream is not available, sour 150 ml/¼ pint/ ⅔ cup single cream by stirring in 5 ml/1 tsp lemon juice and letting the mixture stand until thickened.

Chocolate Sorbet

This velvety smooth sorbet is always popular. Plain dark chocolate gives by far the richest flavour, but if you cannot track this down, then use the very best quality plain dark "Continental" chocolate that you can find or the sorbet will be too sweet.

Serves 6

INGREDIENTS
150 g/5 oz plain dark chocolate, chopped
115 g/4 oz plain chocolate, chopped
200 g/7 oz/1 cup caster sugar
475 ml/16 fl oz/2 cups water
chocolate curls, to decorate

1 Put all the chocolate in a food processor, fitted with the metal blade, and process for 20–30 seconds until finely chopped.

2 Bring the sugar and water to the boil in a saucepan over a medium-high heat, stirring until the sugar dissolves. Boil for about 2 minutes, then remove from the heat.

3 With the machine running, pour the hot syrup over the chocolate. Allow the machine to continue running for 1–2 minutes, until the chocolate is completely melted and the mixture is smooth, scraping down the bowl once.

4 Strain the chocolate mixture into a large measuring jug or bowl, and leave to cool, then chill, stirring occasionally. Freeze the mixture in an ice cream machine, following the manufacturer's instructions. Allow the sorbet to soften for 5–10 minutes at room temperature and serve in scoops, decorated with chocolate curls.

COOK'S TIP: If you do not have an ice cream machine, freeze the sorbet until firm around the edges. Process until smooth, then freeze again.

Rocky Road Ice Cream

This classic sweet ice cream is packed with contrasting textures and flavours.

Serves 6

INGREDIENTS
115 g/4 oz plain chocolate, broken into
    squares
150 ml/¼ pint/⅔ cup milk
300 ml/½ pint/1¼ cups double cream
115 g/4 oz/1½ cups chopped marshmallows
50 g/2 oz/½ cup glacé cherries, chopped
50 g/2 oz/½ cup crumbled
    shortbread biscuits
30 ml/2 tbsp chopped walnuts
chocolate sauce, to serve

1 Melt the plain chocolate in the
milk in a saucepan over a gentle
heat, stirring from time to time.
Remove the pan from the heat and
leave to cool completely.

2 Whip the cream in a bowl until it
just holds its shape. Beat in the
chocolate mixture.

3 Tip the mixture into an ice cream
maker and churn until it is thick
and almost frozen. Alternatively, pour
into a container suitable for use in
the freezer, freeze until ice crystals
form around the edges, then whisk
vigorously until smooth.

4 Stir the marshmallows, cherries,
crushed biscuits and nuts into the
iced mixture, then return to the
freezer container and freeze until firm.
Allow the ice cream to soften at room
temperature for 15-20 minutes before
serving with chocolate sauce.

Chocolate Fudge Sundaes

This self-indulgent American dish is every chocoholic's dream.

Serves 4

INGREDIENTS
4 scoops each vanilla and coffee
   ice cream
2 small ripe bananas
whipped cream
toasted flaked almonds

FOR THE SAUCE
50 g/2 oz/⅓ cup light brown sugar
120 ml/4 fl oz/½ cup golden syrup
45 ml/3 tbsp strong black coffee
5 ml/1 tsp ground cinnamon
150 g/5 oz plain chocolate, chopped into
   small pieces
75 ml/3 fl oz/5 tbsp whipping cream
45 ml/3 tbsp coffee-flavoured liqueur
   (optional)

1 Make the sauce. Place the sugar, syrup, coffee and cinnamon in a heavy-based saucepan. Bring to the boil, then boil for about 5 minutes, stirring the mixture constantly.

2 Turn off the heat and stir in the chocolate. When the chocolate has melted and the mixture is smooth, stir in the cream and the liqueur, if using. Leave the sauce to cool slightly. If made ahead, reheat the sauce gently until just warm.

3 Fill four glasses with a scoop each of vanilla and coffee ice cream. Top with thin slices of banana, warm fudge sauce, whipped cream and toasted almonds. Serve at once.

Chocolate Mousse with Chocolate Curls

Dark, white and milk chocolate curls provide a finishing flourish for a sumptuous chocolate mousse with just a hint of ginger.

Serves 6–8

INGREDIENTS
450 g/1 lb plain chocolate, finely chopped
65 g/2½ oz/5 tbsp butter
200 g/7 oz/scant 1 cup caster sugar
6 eggs, separated
60 ml/4 tbsp ginger syrup
  (from a jar of stem ginger)
100 ml/3½ fl oz/⅓ cup brandy

FOR THE DECORATION
115 g/4 oz plain chocolate or a mixture of
  plain, milk and white chocolate

1 Melt the chocolate and butter with half the sugar in a bowl set over a saucepan of hot water. Remove the bowl from the pan and beat in the egg yolks, ginger syrup and brandy.

2 Whisk the egg whites in a large grease-free bowl until soft peaks form. Gradually add the remaining sugar, a spoonful at a time, whisking constantly until stiff and glossy.

3 Beat about a third of the egg whites into the chocolate mixture to lighten it, then fold in the remainder. Pour into 6–8 serving bowls or glasses and chill for 3–4 hours until set.

4 To make the decoration, melt the chocolate, beat it briefly, then pour on to non-stick baking paper. Spread out with a palette knife until about 3 mm/⅛ in thick. Allow to cool until firm but pliable.

5 For a more dramatic effect make light and dark curls, using plain, milk and white chocolate. Pipe the melted chocolate in alternate rows, smooth each in turn with a palette knife and allow to firm before making the multi-coloured curls.

6 Hold a cheese slicer and place it flat against the chocolate. Pull it gently towards you, scraping off a thin layer of chocolate so that it curls into a scroll. Work quickly or the chocolate will harden and splinter. Decorate the mousses just before serving.

COOK'S TIP: This mousse is an ideal choice when you need a dessert that can be prepared in advance. It can be made up to 3 days before it is needed, provided it is kept in the fridge.

White Amaretto Mousses with Chocolate Sauce

These little white and dark chocolate desserts are extremely rich, and derive their flavour from Amaretto, an almond-flavoured liqueur, and amaretti, little almond-flavoured biscuits.

Serves 8

INGREDIENTS
115 g/4 oz amaretti, ratafia or macaroon biscuits
60 ml/4 tbsp Amaretto liqueur
350 g/12 oz white chocolate, broken into squares
15 g/½ oz powdered gelatine, soaked in 45 ml/3 tbsp cold water
450 ml/¾ pint/scant 2 cups double cream

FOR THE CHOCOLATE SAUCE
225 g/8 oz dark chocolate, broken into squares
300 ml/½ pint/1¼ cups single cream
50 g/2 oz/¼ cup caster sugar

1 Lightly oil eight individual 120 ml/ 4 fl oz moulds and line the base of each mould with a small disc of oiled greaseproof paper. Put the biscuits into a large bowl and crush them finely with the end of a rolling pin.

2 Melt the Amaretto and white chocolate together gently in a bowl over a pan of hot but not boiling water (be very careful not to overheat the chocolate). Stir well until smooth, then remove from the pan and leave to cool.

3 Melt the gelatine over hot water and blend it into the chocolate mixture. Whisk the cream to form soft peaks. Fold in the chocolate mixture, with 60 ml/4 tbsp of the biscuits.

4 Put a teaspoonful of the biscuits into each mould and spoon in the chocolate mixture. Tap to disperse any air bubbles. Level the tops and sprinkle the remaining biscuits on top. Press down and chill for 4 hours.

5 To make the chocolate sauce, put all the ingredients in a small pan and heat gently to melt the chocolate and dissolve the sugar. Simmer for 2–3 minutes. Leave to cool completely.

6 Slip a knife around the sides of each mould, and turn out on to individual plates. Remove the paper, pour a little chocolate sauce around each mousse and serve immediately.

Steamed Chocolate & Fruit Puddings with Chocolate Syrup

Some things always turn out well, including these wonderful little puddings. Dark, fluffy chocolate sponge is topped with tangy cranberries and apple, and served with a honeyed chocolate syrup.

Serves 4

INGREDIENTS

115 g/4 oz/⅔ cup dark muscovado sugar
1 eating apple
75 g/3 oz/¾ cup cranberries, thawed if frozen
115 g/4 oz/8 tbsp soft margarine
2 eggs
75 g/3 oz/⅔ cup plain flour
2.5 ml/½ tsp baking powder
45 ml/3 tbsp cocoa powder

FOR THE CHOCOLATE SYRUP

115 g/4 oz plain chocolate, broken into
   squares
30 ml/2 tbsp clear honey
15 ml/1 tbsp unsalted butter
2.5 ml/½ tsp vanilla essence

1 Prepare a steamer or half fill a saucepan with water and bring it to the boil. Grease four individual pudding basins and sprinkle each one with a little of the muscovado sugar to coat well all over.

2 Peel and core the apple. Dice it into a bowl, add the cranberries and mix well. Divide among the prepared pudding basins.

3 Place the remaining muscovado sugar in a mixing bowl. Add the margarine, eggs, flour, baking powder and cocoa, and beat until combined and smooth.

4 Spoon the mixture into the basins and cover each with a double thickness of foil. Steam for about 45 minutes, topping up the boiling water as required, until the puddings are well risen and firm.

5 Make the syrup. Mix the chocolate, honey, butter and vanilla in a small saucepan. Heat gently, stirring, until melted and smooth.

6 Run a knife around the edge of each pudding to loosen it, then turn out on to individual plates. Serve at once, with the chocolate syrup.

Rich Chocolate Brioche Bake

This scrumptious dessert may be based on bread-and-butter pudding, but chocolate, brioche and marmalade give it superstar status.

Serves 4

INGREDIENTS
200 g/7 oz plain chocolate, broken into
    squares
60 ml/4 tbsp bitter marmalade
45 ml/3 tbsp unsalted butter
4 individual brioches,
    or 1 large brioche loaf
3 eggs
300 ml/½ pint/1¼ cups milk
300 ml/½ pint/1¼ cups single cream
30 ml/2 tbsp demerara sugar

1 Preheat the oven to 180°C/350°F/
Gas 4. Lightly butter a shallow
ovenproof dish and set aside.

2 Melt the chocolate with the
marmalade and butter in a
heatproof bowl over barely simmering
water, stirring the mixture occasionally.

3 Slice the brioche(s), and spread the
melted chocolate mixture over the
slices. Arrange them so that they
overlap in the dish.

4 Beat the eggs, milk and single
cream in a mixing bowl, then pour
the mixture evenly over the brioche
slices. Sprinkle with the demerara
sugar and bake for 40–50 minutes,
until the pudding is lightly set and
bubbling. Serve hot.

Lacy Chocolate Soufflés

A dusting of icing sugar sets off many desserts and cakes. For a special effect, dust through a doily to create a perfect pattern.

Serves 6

INGREDIENTS
175 g/6 oz plain chocolate, chopped
150 g/5 oz/¾ cup unsalted butter, plus extra
   for greasing
4 eggs, separated
30 ml/2 tbsp whisky
50 g/2 oz/¼ cup caster sugar
icing sugar, for dusting

1 Preheat the oven to 220°C/425°F/ Gas 7. Grease six ramekins. Melt the chocolate and butter in a heatproof bowl over hot but not boiling water. Allow to cool slightly, then beat in the egg yolks and whisky.

2 Whisk the egg whites in a large grease-free bowl until soft peaks form. Gradually add the caster sugar, continuing to whisk constantly until stiff and glossy. Beat a third of the whites into the chocolate mixture to lighten it, then fold in the rest.

3 Spoon into the ramekins, place on a baking sheet, and bake for about 10 minutes until well risen.

4 Lay a doily on each individual plate and dust with icing sugar. Do the same with the soufflés, then lift off the doilies and transfer the soufflés to the plates. Serve immediately.

Chocolate Soufflé Crêpes

Use a non-stick pan if possible, and serve two crêpes per person.

Makes 12 crêpes

INGREDIENTS
75 g/3 oz/⅔ cup plain flour
10 g/¼ oz/1 tbsp cocoa powder
5 ml/1 tsp caster sugar
pinch of salt
5 ml/1 tsp ground cinnamon
2 eggs
175 ml/6 fl oz/¾ cup milk
5 ml/1 tsp vanilla essence
50 g/2 oz/4 tbsp unsalted butter, melted
icing sugar for dusting
raspberries, pineapple and mint sprigs
  to decorate

FOR THE PINEAPPLE SYRUP
½ medium pineapple, peeled, cored and
  finely chopped
120 ml/4 fl oz/½ cup water
30 ml/2 tbsp natural maple syrup
5 ml/1 tsp cornflour
½ cinnamon stick
30 ml/2 tbsp rum

FOR THE SOUFFLÉ FILLING
250 g/9 oz plain or plain dark chocolate
75 ml/3 fl oz/⅓ cup double cream
3 eggs, separated
25 g/1 oz/2 tbsp caster sugar

1 Prepare the syrup. Bring the
pineapple, water, maple syrup,
cornflour and cinnamon stick to the
boil over a medium heat. Simmer for
2–3 minutes, whisking frequently.

2 When thickened, remove from the
heat; discard the cinnamon. Pour
into a bowl, stir in the rum and chill.

3 Prepare the crêpes. Sift the flour,
cocoa, sugar, salt and cinnamon
together. Stir, then make a well in the
centre. Beat the eggs, milk and vanilla
and add to the flour mixture to form
a batter. Stir in half the melted butter
and pour into a jug. Let stand 1 hour.

4 Heat an 18–20 cm/7–8 in crêpe
pan. Brush with butter. Stir the
batter, pour 45 ml/3 tbsp into the
pan and swirl to thinly cover the
base. Cook over a medium heat for
1–2 minutes, until the underside is
golden. Turn over and cook for
30–45 seconds. Stack the crêpes
between non-stick baking paper.

5 Prepare the filling. Melt the chocolate and cream in a small saucepan over a medium heat, stirring frequently, until smooth.

6 Using an electric mixer, beat the egg yolks with half the sugar for 3–5 minutes, until creamy. Beat in the chocolate mixture. Beat the whites to soft peaks. Beat in the remaining sugar until stiff peaks form. Beat a spoonful of whites into the cooled chocolate mixture, then fold in the rest.

7 Preheat the oven to 200°C/400°F/ Gas 6. Lay a crêpe on a plate, underside up. Spoon a little soufflé mixture on to the crêpe, spreading it to the edge. Fold the bottom half over the soufflé mixture, then fold in half again to form a filled triangle. Place on a buttered baking sheet. Repeat with the remaining crêpes. Brush the tops with melted butter and bake for 15–20 minutes, until the filling has souffléd. Decorate with raspberries, pineapple, mint and a spoonful of syrup.

Peachy Chocolate Bake

Resist everything except temptation, Oscar Wilde urged. So next time you crave something hot and chocolatey, raid the storecupboard and whip up this delicious pudding.

Serves 6

INGREDIENTS
200 g/7 oz plain dark chocolate, broken into
    squares
115 g/4 oz/½ cup unsalted butter
4 eggs, separated
115 g/4 oz/½ cup caster sugar
425 g/15 oz can peach slices, drained
cream or yogurt, to serve (optional)

4 Fold in large spoonfuls of whisked egg whites, then add the remainder lightly and evenly.

1 Preheat the oven to 160°C/325°F/ Gas 3. Butter a wide ovenproof dish. Melt the chocolate with the butter in a heatproof bowl over barely simmering water. Remove the bowl from the heat.

2 Whisk the egg yolks with the sugar until thick and pale. In a grease-free bowl, whisk the whites until stiff.

3 Beat the melted chocolate into the whisked egg yolk mixture until well combined.

5 Fold the peach slices into the mixture, then tip it carefully into the prepared dish.

6 Bake for 35–40 minutes, or until risen and just firm. Serve hot, with cream or yogurt if liked.

COOK'S TIP: Do not level the mixture as it looks more interesting if the surface is rough and uneven.

Chocolate Roulade

A ravishing roulade topped with curls of fresh coconut, perfect for that special anniversary.

Serves 8

INGREDIENTS
150 g/5 oz/¾ cup caster sugar
5 eggs, separated
50 g/2 oz/½ cup cocoa powder

FOR THE FILLING
300 ml/½ pint/1¼ cups double cream
45 ml/3 tbsp whisky
50 g/2 oz piece solid creamed coconut
25 g/1 oz/2 tbsp caster sugar

FOR THE TOPPING
coarsely grated curls of fresh coconut
chocolate curls

1 Preheat the oven to 180°C/350°F/
Gas 4. Grease and line a 33 x 23
cm/13 x 9 in Swiss roll tin. Dust a
large sheet of greaseproof paper with
30 ml/2 tbsp of the caster sugar.

2 Place the egg yolks in a bowl. Add
the remaining sugar and whisk
with a hand-held electric mixer until
it leaves a trail. Sift the cocoa over,
then fold in carefully.

3 Whisk the egg whites in a clean,
grease-free bowl until they form
soft peaks. Fold about 15 ml/1 tbsp of
the whites into the chocolate mixture
to lighten it, then fold in the
remaining whites evenly.

4 Scrape the mixture into the
prepared tin, taking it right into
the corners. Smooth the surface
with a palette knife, then bake for
20–25 minutes or until well risen
and springy to the touch.

5 Turn the cooked roulade out on to
the sugar-dusted greaseproof paper
and carefully peel off the lining paper.
Cover with a damp, clean tea towel
and leave to cool.

6 Make the filling. Whisk the cream
with the whisky in a bowl until the
mixture just holds its shape, then finely
grate the creamed coconut and stir it
in with the sugar.

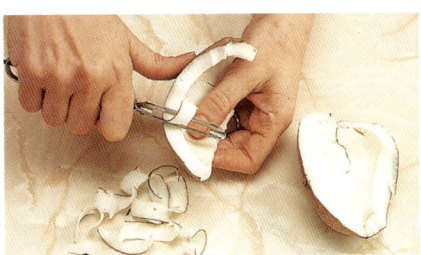

7 Uncover the sponge and spread about three-quarters of the cream mixture to the edges. Roll up carefully from a long side. Transfer to a plate, pipe or spoon the remaining cream mixture on top, then make the coconut curls and place on top with the chocolate curls.

French Chocolate Cake

This very dense chocolate cake can be made up to 3 days before serving, but decorate with icing sugar on the day it is to be served.

Serves 10

INGREDIENTS

250 g/9 oz plain dark chocolate, chopped
225 g/8 oz/1 cup unsalted butter,
   cut into pieces
90 g/3½ oz/½ cup sugar
30 ml/2 tbsp brandy or orange liqueur
5 eggs
15 ml/1 tbsp plain flour
icing sugar, for dusting
whipped or soured cream, to serve

1 Preheat the oven to 180°C/350°F/ Gas 4. Generously grease a 23 x 5 cm/9 x 2 in springform tin. Line the base with non-stick baking paper and grease the paper. Wrap the base and side in foil to keep water out.

2 Melt the chocolate, butter and sugar in a saucepan over a low heat, stirring frequently, until smooth. Cool slightly. Stir in the liqueur. Using an electric mixer, beat the eggs for about 1 minute. Beat in the flour, then slowly beat in the chocolate mixture until well blended. Pour into the tin.

3 Place the tin in a large roasting tin and pour boiling water into the roasting tin to come 2 cm/¾ in up the side. Bake for 25–30 minutes, until the edge of the cake is set, but the centre is still soft to the touch. Remove the tin from the water bath and remove the foil. Cool on a wire rack completely (the cake will sink in the centre and may crack).

4 Carefully run a knife around the edge of the cake. Remove the side of the springform tin and turn the cake on to a wire rack. Remove the springform tin base and the paper, so the bottom of the cake is now the top.

5 Cut 6–8 strips of non-stick baking paper 2.5 cm/1 in wide and place randomly over the cake or make a lattice-style pattern if you prefer. Dust the cake with icing sugar; then carefully remove the paper. Slide the cake on to a serving plate and serve with cream.

Chocolate Pecan Pie

If you thought pecan pie could not be improved upon, just try this gorgeous chocolate one with its rich orange crust.

Serves 6

INGREDIENTS
200 g/7 oz/1¾ cups plain flour
65 g/2½ oz/5 tbsp caster sugar
90 g/3½ oz/scant ½ cup unsalted butter, softened
1 egg, beaten
finely grated rind of 1 orange

FOR THE FILLING
200 g/7 oz/¾ cup golden syrup
45 ml/3 tbsp soft light muscovado sugar
150 g/5 oz plain chocolate, broken into squares
50 g/2 oz/4 tbsp butter
3 eggs, beaten
5 ml/1 tsp vanilla essence
175 g/6 oz/1½ cups pecan nuts

1 Sift the flour into a bowl and stir in the sugar. Work in the butter evenly with the fingertips until well combined.

2 Beat the egg and orange rind in a bowl, then stir into the mixture to make a firm dough. Add a little water if the mixture is too dry.

3 Roll out the pastry on a lightly floured surface and use to line a deep, 20 cm/8 in loose-based flan tin. Chill for 30 minutes.

4 Preheat the oven to 180°C/350°F/Gas 4. Make the pie filling. Mix the golden syrup, muscovado sugar, chocolate and butter in a small saucepan. Heat the mixture gently until it is melted and smooth.

5 Remove the pan from the heat and beat in the eggs and the vanilla essence. Sprinkle the pecan nuts into the chilled pastry case and carefully pour in the melted chocolate mixture.

6 Place the pie on a baking sheet and bake for 50–60 minutes, or until the chocolate mixture is set. Cool completely in the tin.

COOK'S TIP: Make individual tartlets if you prefer – use six 10 cm/4 in flan tins and bake at the same temperature for about 30 minutes. Walnuts or almonds can be used instead of pecan nuts.

Luxury White Cheesecake

An unusual version of a traditional baked cheesecake.

Serves 16–20

INGREDIENTS
150 g/5 oz (about 16–18) digestive biscuits
65 g/2½ oz/½ cup blanched
    hazelnuts, toasted
50 g/2 oz/4 tbsp unsalted butter,
    melted
2.5 ml/½ tsp ground cinnamon

FOR THE FILLING
350 g/12 oz fine quality white
    chocolate, chopped
120 ml/4 fl oz/½ cup whipping or double
    cream
675 g/1½ lb/3 x 8 oz packets cream
    cheese, softened
50 g/2 oz/¼ cup sugar
4 eggs
30 ml/2 tbsp hazelnut-flavour liqueur
    or 15 ml/1 tbsp vanilla essence

FOR THE TOPPING
450 ml/¾ pint/scant 2 cups soured cream
50 g/2 oz/¼ cup sugar
15 ml/1 tbsp hazelnut-flavour liqueur or
    5 ml/1 tsp vanilla essence
white chocolate curls, to decorate
cocoa powder, for dusting (optional)

1 Preheat the oven to 180°C/350°F/
Gas 4. Lightly grease a 23 x 7.5 cm/
9 x 3 in springform tin. In a food
processor, process the biscuits and
hazelnuts until fine crumbs form.
Add the butter and cinnamon.

2 Using a spoon, press on to the base
to within 1 cm/½ in of the top of
the tin. Bake for 5–7 minutes, until
just set. Remove to a rack to cool.
Lower the oven temperature to
150°C/300°F/Gas 2.

3 Melt the white chocolate and
cream in a saucepan over a low
heat, stirring until smooth. Set aside.

4 Using an electric mixer, beat the
cream cheese and sugar for 2–4
minutes, until smooth. Beat in the
eggs, one at a time. Slowly add the
chocolate mixture and liqueur or
vanilla essence. Pour the filling into
the baked crust.

5 Place the tin on a baking sheet.
Bake for 45–55 minutes, or until
the edge of the cake is firm but the
centre is still slightly soft, but do not
allow it to brown. Remove to a rack
while preparing the topping. Increase
the oven to 200°C/400°F/Gas 6.

6 To make the topping, whisk the soured cream, sugar and liqueur or vanilla together. Pour over the cheesecake, and return to the oven. Bake for 5–7 minutes. Turn off the oven and leave for 1 hour. Remove to a rack until at room temperature. Run a knife around the edge. Refrigerate, loosely covered, overnight.

7 To serve the cheesecake, gently remove the side of the springform tin. Slide a sharp knife under the crust to separate it from the base and, with a metal palette knife, slide carefully on to a serving plate. Decorate the cake with white chocolate curls and dust lightly with cocoa powder, if liked. Serve immediately.

Chocolate Pavlova with Chocolate Curls & Fruits

The addition of chocolate to the traditional fruit makes this popular dessert even harder to resist.

Serves 8–10

INGREDIENTS
275 g/10 oz/2¼ cups icing sugar
10 g/¼ oz/1 tbsp cocoa powder
5 ml/1 tsp cornflour
5 egg whites at room temperature
pinch of salt
5 ml/1 tsp cider vinegar or
    lemon juice

FOR THE CHOCOLATE CREAM
175 g/6 oz plain or plain dark chocolate,
    chopped
120 ml/4 fl oz//½ cup milk
25 g/1 oz/2 tbsp unsalted butter,
    cut into pieces
30 ml/2 tbsp brandy
475 ml/16 fl oz/2 cups double or
    whipping cream

FOR THE TOPPING
chocolate curls
450 g/1 lb/2 cups mixed berries or cut-up
    fruits, such as mango, papaya, fresh
    lychees and pineapple
icing sugar

1 Prepare the meringue. Preheat the oven to 160°C/325°F/Gas 3. Place a sheet of non-stick baking paper on a large baking sheet and mark a 20 cm/8 in circle on it.

2 In a bowl, sift 3 tbsp of icing sugar with the cocoa and cornflour. Using an electric mixer, beat the egg whites until frothy. Add the salt and beat until stiff peaks form. Gradually sprinkle in the remaining icing sugar, pausing to let it dissolve. Fold in the sugar mixture, then the vinegar or lemon juice.

3 Spoon the mixture on to the circle on the paper, building up the sides. Bake in the centre of the oven for 1 hour, until set. Turn off the oven and allow the meringue to stand in the oven for 1 hour (it may crack or sink). Remove and cool.

4 Melt the chocolate and milk in a saucepan over a low heat, stirring until smooth. Off the heat, whisk in the butter and brandy and cool for 1 hour.

5 Using a palette knife, transfer the meringue to a serving plate. Cut a circle around the centre, about 5 cm/ 2 in from the edge to allow it to sink. When the chocolate mixture has cooled, but is not too firm, beat the cream until soft peaks form. Stir half the cream into the chocolate, then fold in the rest. Spoon into the centre of the meringue. Arrange chocolate curls and berries or fruits on top. Dust lightly with icing sugar.

Chocolate Mandarin Trifle

Trifle is always a tempting treat, but when a rich chocolate and mascarpone custard is combined with Amaretto and mandarin oranges, it becomes sheer delight.

Serves 6–8

INGREDIENTS
4 trifle sponges
14 amaretti biscuits
60 ml/4 tbsp Amaretto liqueur or
    sweet sherry
8 mandarin oranges

FOR THE CUSTARD
200 g/7 oz plain chocolate, broken
    into squares
25 g/1 oz/2 tbsp cornflour or custard powder
25 g/1 oz/2 tbsp caster sugar
2 egg yolks
200 ml/7 fl oz/scant 1 cup milk
250 g/9 oz/generous 1 cup mascarpone

FOR THE TOPPING
250 g/9 oz/generous 1 cup fromage frais
chocolate shapes
mandarin slices

1 Break up the trifle sponges and place them in a large glass serving dish. Crumble the amaretti biscuits over and then sprinkle with Amaretto or sweet sherry.

2 Squeeze the juice from 2 mandarins and sprinkle into the dish. Segment the rest of the mandarins and put in the dish in an even layer.

3 Make the custard. Melt the chocolate in a heatproof bowl over hot water. In a separate bowl, mix the cornflour or custard powder, sugar and egg yolks to a paste.

4 Heat the milk in a small saucepan until almost boiling, then pour on to the egg yolk mixture, stirring constantly. Return to the clean pan and keep stirring over a low heat until the custard has thickened slightly and is smooth.

5 Stir in the mascarpone until melted, then add the melted chocolate, mixing it evenly. Spread evenly over the trifle, cool, then chill until set.

6 To finish, spread the fromage frais over the custard, then decorate with chocolate shapes and mandarin slices just before serving.

Chocolate Profiteroles

Light-as-air choux pastry puffs are filled with ice cream and coated with a rich chocolate sauce.

Serves 4–6

INGREDIENTS
110 g/3¾ oz/scant 1 cup plain flour
1.5 ml/¼ tsp salt
pinch of freshly grated nutmeg
175 ml/6 fl oz/¾ cup water
75 g/3 oz/6 tbsp unsalted butter, cut into
    6 equal pieces
3 eggs
750 ml/1¼ pints/3 cups vanilla ice cream

FOR THE CHOCOLATE SAUCE
275 g/10 oz plain chocolate, chopped into
    small pieces
120 ml/4 fl oz/½ cup warm water

1 Preheat the oven to 200°C/
400°F/Gas 6. Grease a baking
sheet. Sift the flour, salt and freshly
grated nutmeg on to a sheet of non-
stick baking paper or foil.

2 Make the sauce. Melt the chocolate
with the water in a heatproof bowl
placed over a saucepan of barely
simmering water. Stir until smooth.
Keep warm until ready to serve, or
reheat when required.

3 In a medium saucepan, bring the
water and butter to the boil.
Remove from the heat and add the
dry ingredients all at once, funnelling
them in from the paper or foil.

4 Beat with a wooden spoon for
about 1 minute, until well blended
and starting to pull away from the
sides of the pan. Set the pan over a
low heat and cook the mixture for
about 2 minutes, beating constantly.
Remove from the heat.

5 Beat 1 egg in a small bowl and set
aside. Add the whole eggs, one at a
time, to the flour mixture, beating
vigorously after each addition. Beat in
just enough of the beaten egg to make
a smooth, shiny dough. It should pull
away and fall slowly when dropped
from a spoon.

6 Using a tablespoon, ease the dough
in 12 mounds on to the prepared
baking sheet. Bake for 25–30 minutes,
until the puffs are golden brown.
Remove the puffs from the oven and
cut a small slit in the side of each to
release the steam. Return to the oven,
turn off the heat and leave them to
dry out, with the oven door open.

7 Remove the ice cream from the freezer and allow it to soften for about 10 minutes. Split the profiteroles in half and put a small scoop of ice cream in each. Arrange on a serving platter or divide among individual plates. Pour the sauce over the profiteroles and serve at once.

VARIATION: The profiteroles can be filled with whipped cream instead of ice cream, if you prefer. Either spoon the cream into a piping bag and fill the slit profiteroles, or halve them and sandwich them together with the whipped cream.

Chocolate Truffles

Truffles can be simply dusted with cocoa, icing sugar, finely chopped nuts or coated in melted chocolate.

Makes 20 large or 30 medium truffles

INGREDIENTS
250 ml/8 fl oz/1 cup double cream
275 g/10 oz fine quality plain or plain dark chocolate, chopped
40 g/1½ oz/3 tbsp unsalted butter, cut into small pieces
45 ml/3 tbsp brandy, whisky or other liqueur

TO FINISH (OPTIONAL)
cocoa powder for dusting
finely chopped pistachios
400 g/14 oz plain dark chocolate
crystallised ginger, chopped

1 Bring the cream to the boil in a saucepan over a medium heat. Remove from the heat and add the chocolate all at once. Stir gently until melted. Stir in the butter until melted, then stir in the brandy, whisky or liqueur. Strain into a bowl and cool to room temperature. Cover and refrigerate for 4 hours or overnight.

2 Using an ice cream scoop, melon baller or tablespoon, scrape up the mixture into 20 large or 30 medium balls and place on a baking sheet lined with non-stick baking paper.

3 If dusting with cocoa, sift a thick layer of cocoa on to a dish or pie plate. Roll the truffles in cocoa, rounding them between the palms of your hands. (Dust your hands with cocoa to prevent the truffles from sticking.) Do not worry if the truffles are not perfectly round, as the irregular shape looks more authentic.

4 Alternatively, roll in very finely chopped pistachios. Refrigerate the truffles for up to 10 days or freeze them for up to 2 months.

5 If coating with chocolate, do not roll in cocoa or nuts, but coat with chocolate melted by the direct heat method and refrigerate immediately. Melt the chocolate in a small bowl. Using a fork, dip the truffles into the melted chocolate, one at a time, tapping the fork on the edge of the bowl to shake off excess. If the chocolate begins to thicken, reheat gently until smooth.

6 Place the finished truffles on a baking sheet lined with non-stick baking paper. Refrigerate until set.

Hot White Chocolate

Use milk or plain chocolate, plus sugar, if you prefer.

Serves 4

INGREDIENTS
175 g/6 oz white chocolate
1.5 litres/2½ pints/6¼ cups milk
5 ml/1 tsp coffee essence, or 10 ml/2 tsp instant coffee powder
10 ml/2 tsp orange-flavoured liqueur (optional)

FOR SERVING
whipped cream
ground cinnamon (optional)

1 With a sharp knife, finely chop the white chocolate. (Try not to handle it too much.)

2 Pour the milk into a medium-sized heavy saucepan and bring just to the boil (bubbles will form around the edge of the pan).

3 Add the chopped white chocolate, coffee essence or powder, and orange-flavoured liqueur, if using. Stir until the chocolate has melted.

4 Divide the hot chocolate among 4 coffee mugs. Top each with a rosette of whipped cream and a sprinkling of ground cinnamon, if using. Serve immediately.

Easy Chocolate Hazelnut Fudge

Giftwrap this delicious fudge for an ideal handmade present.

Makes 16 squares

INGREDIENTS
150 ml/¼ pint/⅔ cup evaporated milk
350 g/12 oz/1¾ cups sugar
pinch of salt
50 g/2 oz/½ cup halved hazelnuts
350 g/12 oz/2 cups plain chocolate chips
5 ml/1 tsp hazelnut liqueur (optional)

1 Generously grease a 20 cm/8 in square cake tin. Combine the evaporated milk, sugar and salt in a heavy saucepan. Bring to the boil over a medium heat, stirring constantly. Simmer the mixture gently, continuing to stir, for about 5 minutes.

2 Remove from the heat and add the halved hazelnuts, chocolate chips, and hazelnut liqueur, if using. Stir until the chocolate chips have completely melted.

3 Quickly pour the fudge mixture into the prepared tin and spread it out evenly, using a metal palette knife. Allow to cool completely.

4 When the fudge is set, cut into 2.5 cm/1 in squares. Store in an airtight container, separating the layers with non-stick baking paper.